The Usborne Chess Book

Lucy Bowman

Chess consultant: Richard James

Illustrated by Candice Whatmore
Designed by Michael Hill
Edited by Kirsteen Robson and Sam Taplin

Usborne Quicklinks

There are lots of good websites where you
can find out more about how to play chess. To find
links to websites where you can watch video clips,
follow step-by-step lessons and improve your chess skills
with puzzles and games, go to the Usborne Quicklinks
website at **www.usborne.com/quicklinks**
and type in the name of this book.

Internet safety

Please follow the internet safety guidelines
displayed at the Usborne Quicklinks website. You'll
find more tips and advice on staying safe on the internet
there too. We recommend that young children are
supervised while using the internet.

The websites recommended at Usborne Quicklinks are
regularly reviewed and updated but Usborne Publishing
is not responsible for the content or availability
of any website other than its own.

About this book

The activities in this book will teach you
the basics of chess, test your understanding and
improve your skills. For some activities you may find
it useful to have a chessboard in front of you, so you
can move pieces around before answering the puzzles.
Some of the puzzles are answered using stickers,
which you can find at the back of the book. You'll find
the answers to all the puzzles at the back, too.

If you're new to chess, try the activities
in the order they appear in the book so
you can learn how to play the game
as you go along.

Pawn   Pawn   Pawn   Pawn   Pawn   Pawn   Pawn   Pawn

Rook   Knight   Bishop   Queen   King   Bishop   Knight   Rook

Chess basics

Chess is a game for two, played on a board with 64 squares. The squares and pieces are described as black and white, but they can be any light and dark shade. Each player starts the game with 16 pieces.

1 king   1 queen   2 bishops   2 knights   2 rooks   8 pawns

Piece moves

The pieces move in different ways. Read the description for each piece, then draw on more spots and arrows to show every move that piece can make.

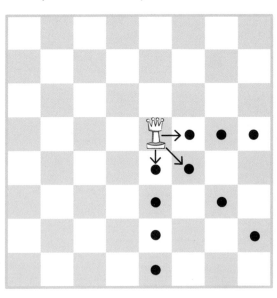

Kings move one square in any direction, but not onto a square where they could be captured.

Queens can move in a straight line in any direction, across any number of empty squares.

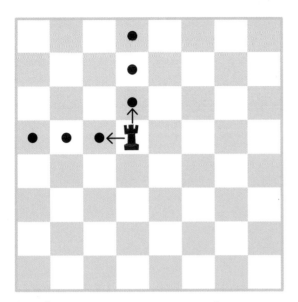

Rooks can move any number of empty squares forwards, backwards or sideways.

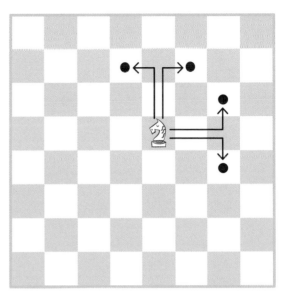

Knights move in an 'L' shape, like this. They are the only pieces that can jump over other pieces.

I'll travel on the black squares and you can move on the white ones.

Bishops move diagonally over any number of empty squares. One of a player's bishops travels only on white squares, the other on black.

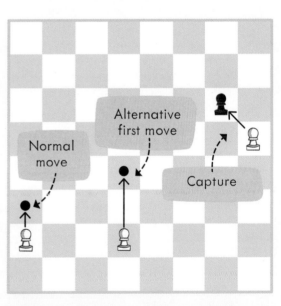

Alternative first move

Normal move

Capture

Pawns move forwards, usually one square at a time. However, on their first move they can move two squares. To capture*, they move forwards one square diagonally.

* To find out more about captures, see the short rules of chess on page 8.

5

Setting up the board

At the start of the game, the pieces are arranged in two rows at either end of the board, with the black and white pieces mirroring each other. Add black piece stickers to finish setting up the board below.

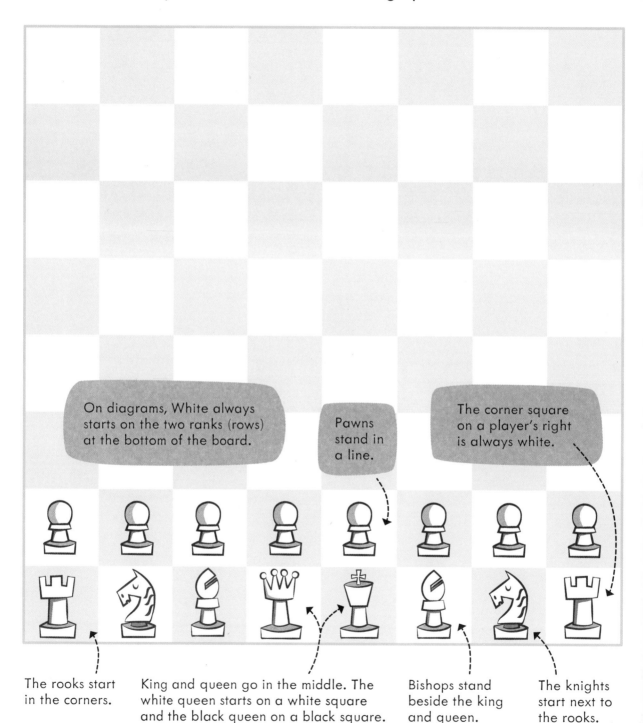

On diagrams, White always starts on the two ranks (rows) at the bottom of the board.

Pawns stand in a line.

The corner square on a player's right is always white.

The rooks start in the corners.

King and queen go in the middle. The white queen starts on a white square and the black queen on a black square.

Bishops stand beside the king and queen.

The knights start next to the rooks.

Misplaced pieces

Circle the pieces that are in the wrong place on these boards.

1

2

Remember, I always match my starting square.

Areas of the board

Each part of the board has its own name. Read the descriptions below, then write letters on to label the areas of the boards.

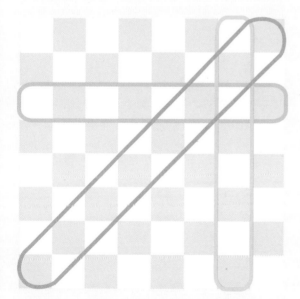

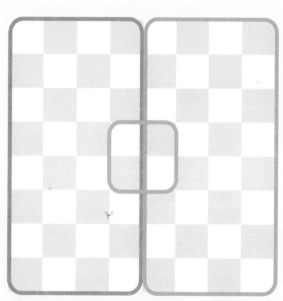

Rank (R) – a row of squares (across)

File (F) – a column of squares (up and down)

Diagonal (D) – a line of diagonal squares

Kingside (K) – the four files on the kings' side of the board

Queenside (Q) – the four files on the queens' side of the board

Central squares (C) – the four middle squares

7

Chess - the short rules

- White always starts.

- Players take turns to move one of their pieces.

- A piece that moves to the square of an opponent's piece captures that piece. Captured pieces are taken off the board.

- Try to capture your opponent's pieces while keeping your own pieces safe – the more powerful your army, the easier it is to win.

- You win the game by trapping your opponent's king. This is called checkmate. (You can find out more about this on page 10.)

I'll have that square, please.

And that's checkmate...

Controlling the board

A piece controls any squares it can capture other pieces on. Write W or B on any empty squares that White or Black control.

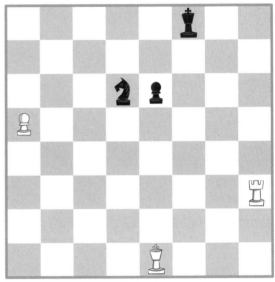

Capture!

Draw arrows on the board below to show all the captures that White could make next. One has been drawn for you.

Piece codes

All pieces except pawns have their own letter and symbol.

I don't have my own letter.

King   Queen   Rook   Bishop   Knight   Pawn

Board codes

The ranks on a chessboard are numbered 1 to 8, and the files are lettered a to h. White's pieces always start on ranks 1 and 2, and Black's begin on 7 and 8. Each square has its own code. A square's code is the letter of its file, followed by the number of its rank.

Write in the missing codes on this chessboard.

8	a8		c8	d8	e8	f8	g8	
7		b7	c7	d7		f7	g7	h7
6	a6	b6		d6	e6		g6	h6
5		b5	c5	d5	e5	f5		h5
4	a4	b4	c4		e4	f4	g4	
3	a3			d3	e3	f3	g3	h3
2	a2	b2	c2	d2			g2	h2
1	a1	b1	c1		e1	f1		h1
	a	b	c	d	e	f	g	h

Pieces in place

A piece code followed by a square code shows where a piece is on the board. This book's answer pages often use these written codes. Write down the codes for the pieces below and the squares they are on, starting with the queen in file a.

Qa5 ....

....

8					♚			
7							♟	
6			♞					
5	♛							
4				♕				
3						♘		
2		♗						
1								♖
	a	b	c	d	e	f	g	h

The king

The king is the most important piece, though not the most powerful. If it is trapped and can't escape, the game is over and the opposing player has won.

Check and checkmate

When a king is under attack (on a square in its enemy's control*), it is in *check*. If your king is in check your next move must be to stop the check. If you can't stop a check, this is *checkmate* and you have lost.

Ways to escape check

- Capture the checking piece.
- Move your king out of check.
- Place another piece between the attacking piece and your king (this doesn't work when a knight attacks).

1 Add a black knight sticker below to put the white king in check.

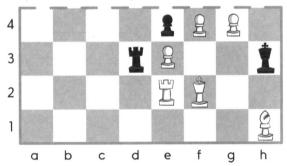

2 Add a black queen sticker below to put the white king in checkmate.

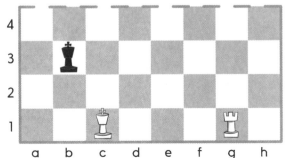

3 Add a black bishop sticker below to put the white king in checkmate.

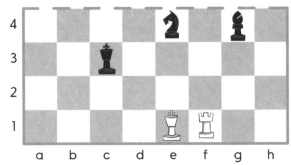

* For more about controlling squares, see page 8.

King on the run

Draw a line to show the black king's route to escape from the top-left corner of the chessboard to the bottom-right corner, avoiding check. (Only the king can move in this puzzle, and it can't capture.)

REMEMBER:
The king can only move one square at a time.

You can't use that square – you're in check.

Check and checkmate puzzles

Try these puzzles to test your understanding of the rules of check and checkmate.

FACT: It's illegal to play a move that leaves your king in check. If you do, you must take back your move and play another instead.

Hold on – your king's in check.

Check escape

Getting your king out of check is just as important as knowing how to trap your opponent's king. Draw an arrow on each board below to help the white king escape check.

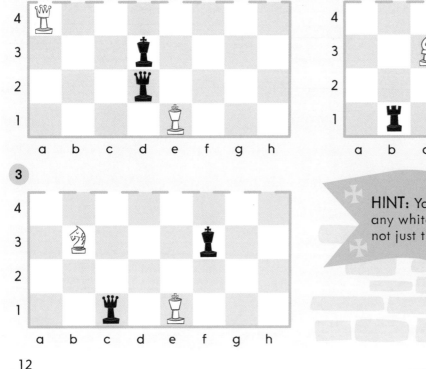

1

2

3

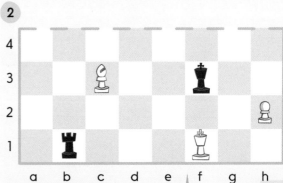

HINT: You can move any white piece, not just the king...

Checkmate challenges

Add the following white piece stickers to each of these boards to put the black king in checkmate:

1 white queen

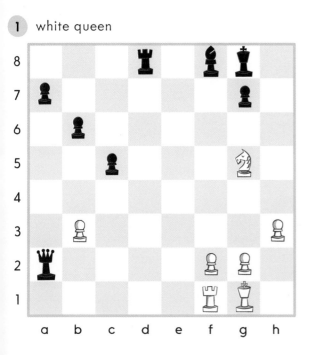

2 white rook

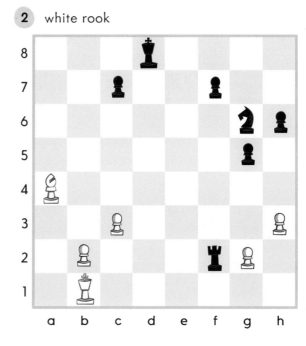

3 white bishop

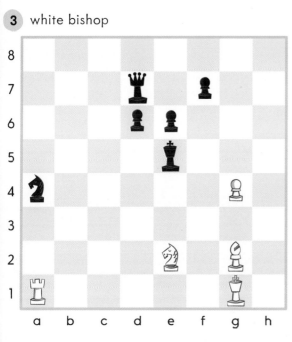

4 white knight

More checkmate challenges

Can you place a white king sticker on each of these boards, so that White is in checkmate?

REMEMBER: In these challenges, the white king can't go on a square next to the black king, because then Black would be in check.

You can't stand there – you're in check!

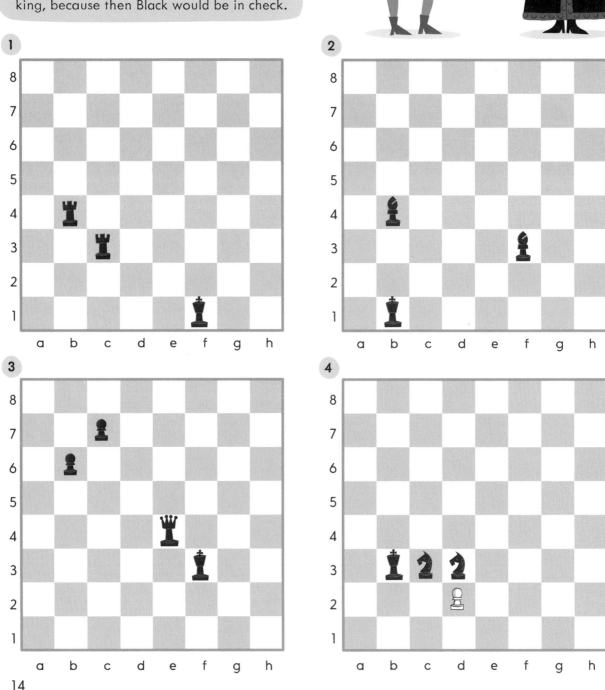

Stalemate

If you can't move any pieces, and you're not in check, you are in *stalemate.* When either player ends up in stalemate, the game is a draw*.

The white king is in stalemate in both positions below – it's not in check and it can't move.

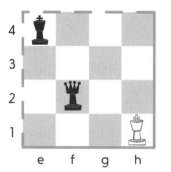

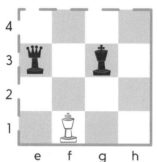

I guess I'm stuck here.

But we were winning!

Which is which?

It's White's turn. Write above each board whether it shows check, checkmate, or stalemate.

TIP: If your opponent only has a king left, be careful not to put it in stalemate – otherwise the game will be a draw.

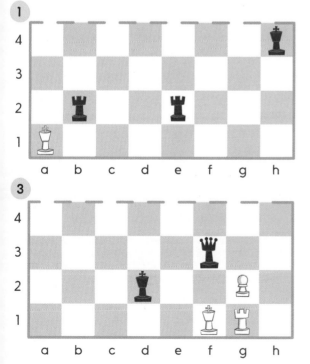

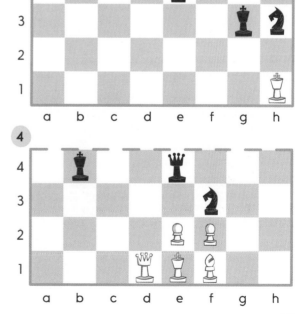

* You can find out more about drawn games on pages 50-51.

The rook

Each player has two rooks. They can move any number of squares in a straight line.

Some people nickname us castles.

Rook checkmate

Rooks are very useful for putting your opponent's king in checkmate. Add a white rook sticker to each board to put Black's king in checkmate.

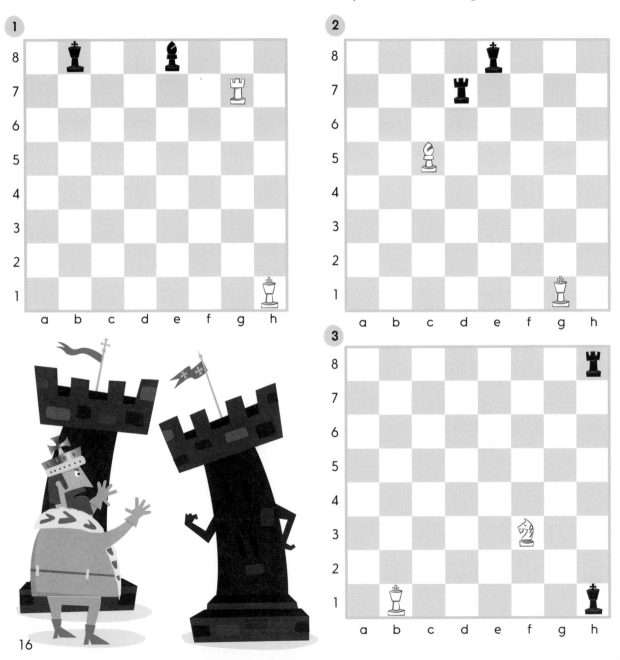

Rook threats

On each of these boards, which square can the black rook move to that threatens two white pieces at once? Use an arrow to show the move.

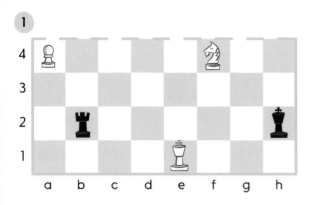

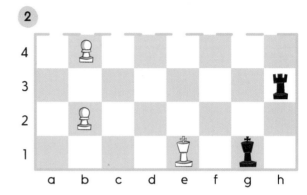

Rook attack

Find a route for Black's rook to capture every white piece on the board on the right. It must take a piece on every move, and finish by capturing White's king. (The white pieces don't move.)

TIP: Rooks are valuable pieces. Don't bring them out too soon. Your opponent may use weaker pieces, such as bishops and knights, to chase them around the board, which will waste your moves.

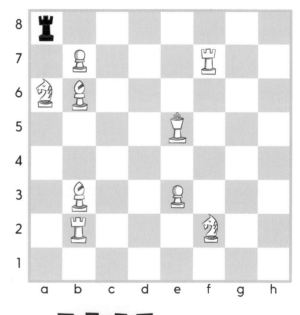

17

Under attack

Rooks can't move diagonally, and so they are open to diagonal attacks. Draw an arrow on each board to show White's move that would threaten a black rook diagonally.

1

2

3

TIP: Rooks struggle to move at the start because they are trapped by their own pieces. They're usually more useful later on when the board has more spaces.

Rook positions

Which player has the better positioned rooks on this board? Write Black or White on the board to show your answer.

Teamwork

Rooks work well as a team. Add a white rook sticker to each of these boards to put the black kings in checkmate.

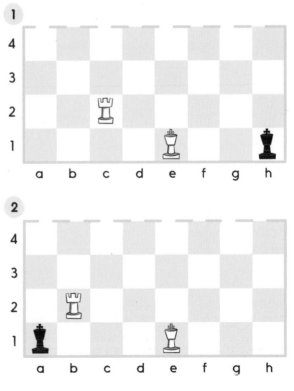

There are two possible answers to this puzzle.

The bishop

Each player has two bishops – one that travels on white squares and one that moves on black.

Board control

The numbers on this chessboard show how many squares the bishop can control from each position. Can you fill in all the missing numbers?

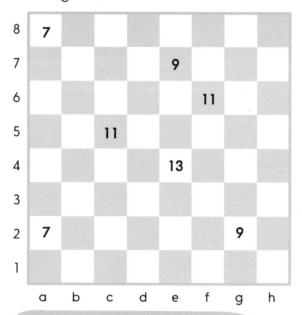

TIP: If your opponent has only one bishop left, your pieces are safe from it if they stay on squares of the opposite shade to the one it's on.

You can't catch me on the white squares.

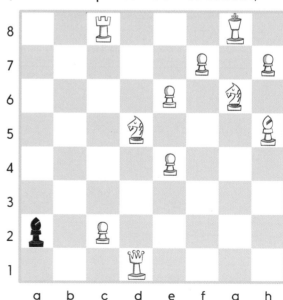

FACT: Each bishop can only land on half the squares on the board.

I can land on every single square on the board.

Show off...

Piece collecting

Draw the black bishop's route so it can capture all the white pieces, in as few moves as possible. (The other pieces do not move.)

20

Bishop checkmates

Add two white bishop stickers to each of these boards to put the black king in checkmate.

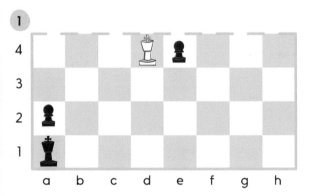

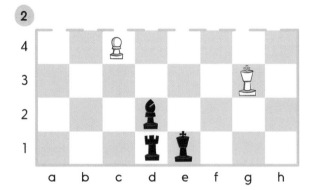

Draw an arrow on each of these boards showing the move the black bishop can make to put the white king in checkmate.

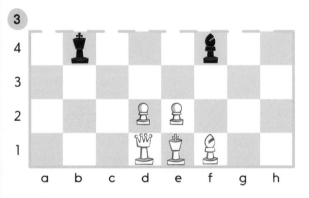

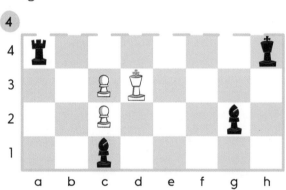

Coming through!

TIP: It's usually a good idea to bring your bishops out early, to control as many squares as possible.

21

The queen

The queen is the most powerful piece because it can move any number of squares in any direction.

You can't run from me.

We know, Your Majesty.

Queen in control

The numbers on this chessboard show how many squares the queen can control from each position. Can you fill in all the missing numbers?

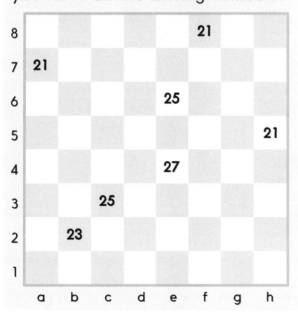

Queen attack

Which pieces could the white queen capture on the board below? Draw circles around them.

Queen attacked

Can this black queen escape capture? Add a ✓ or a ✗ sticker on the yellow square to show your answer.

22

TIP: Queens are good at taking pieces by surprise, as they can swoop in from the other end of the board in more than one direction.

Boo!

ARGH!

Queen checkmates

The queen is an important checkmating tool. Add a black queen sticker to each board below to put the white king in checkmate.

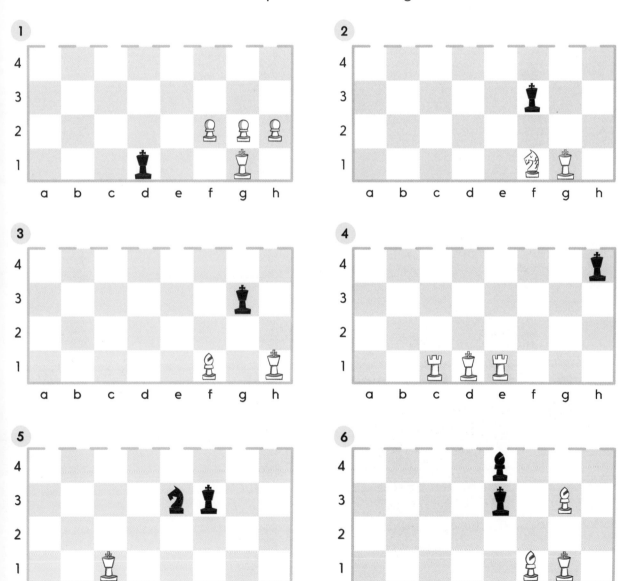

Queen forks

A piece can *fork* its opponent's pieces – this means that it threatens two or more pieces at once. Queens are good at forking because they can threaten lots of squares at the same time. Add a white queen sticker to each board to fork the black king and either a black rook or a black bishop. Make sure the queen is on a safe square.

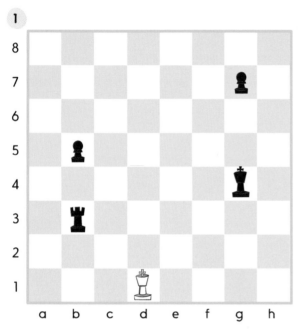

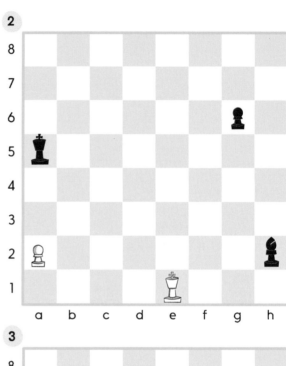

Gotcha!

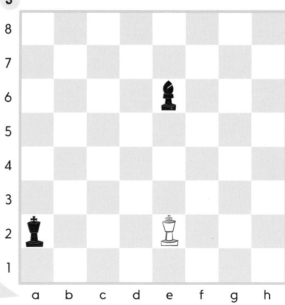

24

Runaway queen

This white queen is at risk of capture and only one square is safe. Draw an arrow showing its move from danger.

King and queen checkmate

Sometimes the last three pieces left will be your king and queen, and your opponent's king. To checkmate your opponent, use your queen to force your opponent's king to the edge of the board. Your king can then take control of the only escape squares while the queen forces checkmate. What move can Black's queen make below to put White's king in checkmate? Draw it on with an arrow.

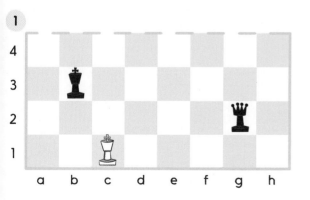

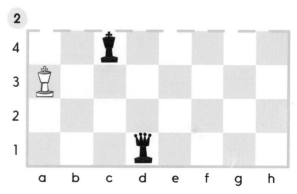

There are two possible answers to this puzzle.

The knight

Each player has two knights. They move in an L-shape (see page 5).

Count the moves

Starting on d5, what is the smallest number of moves this black knight will take to reach each square on the board below? Write the number of moves on the rest of the squares.

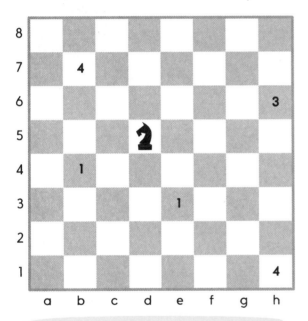

FACT: Knights can jump over other pieces, making it easy to bring them into play at the start of the game.

Knight tour challenge

When you first play chess, it's easy to misjudge and land a knight on the wrong square in an illegal move.

Get used to moving the knight correctly by trying to land just once on every square below. Use a pencil to draw lines, and spots to show where each move starts and finishes. The first three moves have been drawn for you.

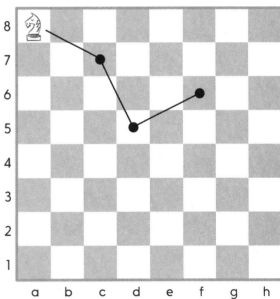

HINT: There is more than one right answer to this puzzle – but it's very tricky, even for advanced chess players. You have done very well if you can land the knight on 50 squares.

Knight journeys

What is the smallest number of moves it takes for each white knight to capture the black pawn? Write your answers under the boards.

1

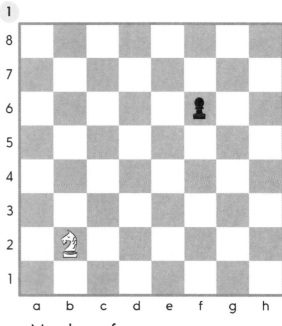

Number of moves ....

In control

How many squares can a knight control from each square on the board? Fill in the missing numbers.

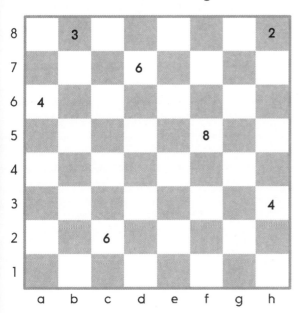

2

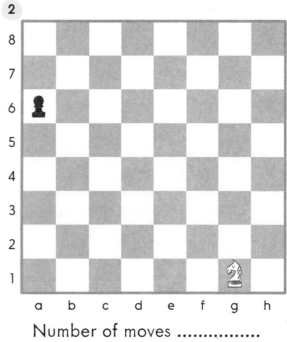

Number of moves ....

27

Knight captures

Use circles and arrows to show all the pieces that each knight could capture on its next move. (One capture has been shown for you.)

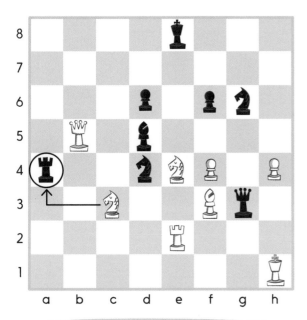

> **TIP:** Knights are good at forking (attacking two or more pieces) because they can attack in eight different directions.

Watch out – all of you...

Sneaky forks

Can you place a white knight sticker on each board below to fork two black pieces (threaten them at the same time)?

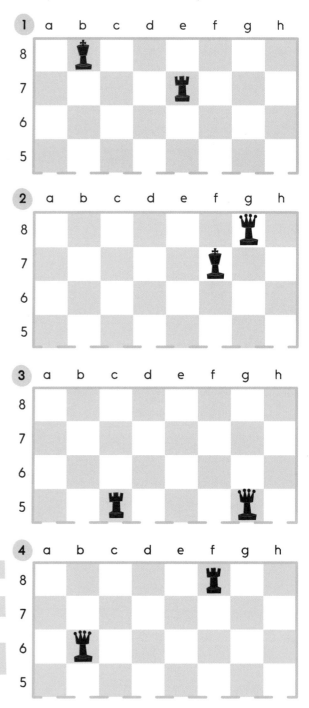

Checkmates

Place two white knight stickers on each of the boards below to put the black king in checkmate.

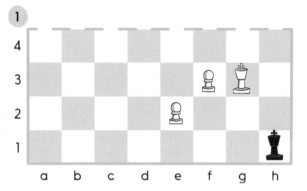

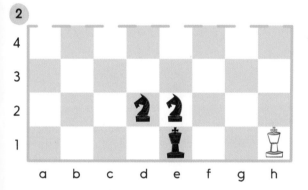

Getting to the middle

Can either knight reach the middle square? They can move as many times as you want within the nine squares. Draw a ✓ in the box next to your answer.

Yes

No

Safe knight

How many safe single moves can Black make to protect the knight from attack, without moving the knight itself? Use arrows to show them.

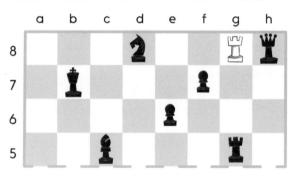

Trapped knight

All four knights on this board are in danger of being captured – but only one can't move to safety. Draw a circle around the trapped knight.

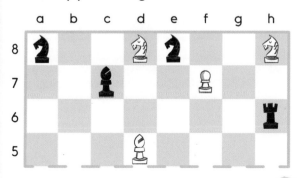

I'm safest on squares that are defended by one of my own pawns.

I've got you covered!

The pawns

Players start the game with eight pawns each. They are the least powerful pieces, but they have some very important uses.

Pawn protectors

Pawns are good at keeping more valuable pieces safe. Add a white pawn sticker and a black pawn sticker to each of these boards where they will protect pieces in danger of being captured.

REMEMBER: Pawns can't move backwards – so think carefully before you move them forwards.

Once I move there's no going back.

En passant

The *en passant* rule allows a pawn to make a special move. If a pawn moves forwards two squares on its first turn, and passes a square controlled by its opponent's pawn, that pawn can capture it anyway. The move looks like this:

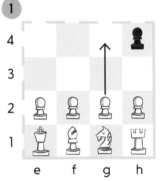

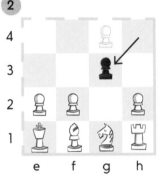

1. The white pawn moves forwards two squares to g4, sneaking past g3.

2. But Black's pawn moves to g3 (the square it controlled), and captures the g4 pawn.

Ha ha! You forgot the *en passant* rule, didn't you? Off you go!

Quick pawn quiz

1. **How many squares can a pawn move on its first turn?**
   a. one square
   b. two squares
   c. either one or two squares

2. **A pawn captures by moving:**
   a. one square forwards
   b. one square diagonally forwards
   c. one square backwards

3. **At the start of a game of chess, each player has:**
   a. two pawns
   b. four pawns
   c. eight pawns

4. **When you make an *en passant* capture...**

   ...your pawn starts on:
   a. the same file as your opponent's pawn
   b. the next file to your opponent's pawn

   ...your opponent's pawn has just moved:
   a. one square
   b. two squares

   ...your pawn ends up on:
   a. the square the other pawn moved from
   b. the square the other pawn passed over
   c. the square the other pawn moved to

Pawn promotion

If one of your pawns reaches the last rank at the opposite end of the board, it is immediately promoted. This means you can replace it with any piece, except a king, even if you already have one or more of those pieces on the board.

Players usually choose to promote to a queen, but sometimes a trade for a less powerful piece is even better. (A knight can reach squares on its first move that a queen can't, and a queen may put its opponent in stalemate*.)

It is White's turn to move below.
Should White promote the pawns
to bishops, knights, rooks or queens?
Write your answer on each board.

TIP: Think carefully about which piece to promote to, even though a queen is usually the best choice.

Pick me!

But my move is unique.

Me! Me!

* To read about stalemate, see page 15.

Pawn checkmates

The white kings below are almost in checkmate, but in every case a pawn is missing. Use a black pawn sticker to seal each king's doom.

1

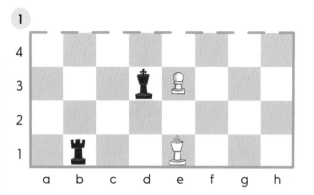

2

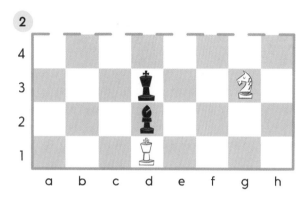

3

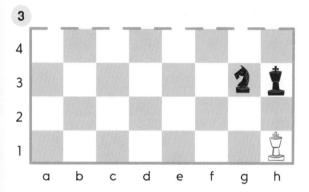

There are two possible answers to this puzzle.

4

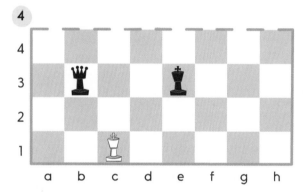

Think ahead

What is the best move that White can make here? Think carefully about Black's next move before you decide, then draw White's move on with an arrow.

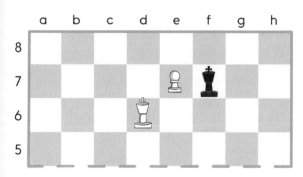

TIP: If a king stands to the side of one of its pawns, it can protect the pawn as it moves towards promotion.

I'll take care of you.

Castling

Castling is a useful move that hides your king safely behind its pawns, and moves your rook to the middle, to attack more easily along files with no pawns on them.

It works like this:

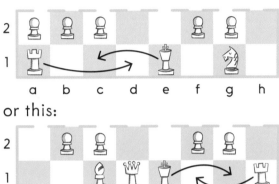

or this:

Rule breakers?

White has just castled on the two boards below. Add a ✗ sticker if the castling rules have been broken and a ✓ sticker if they have been kept.

1

2

Freedom!

Safe at last.

TIP: It's a good idea to castle early in the game, so that your king is protected and one of your rooks isn't stuck in the corner of the board.

To castle or not to castle?

On one of these boards, Black should castle; on the other, it definitely should not. Add a ✓ or a ✗ sticker on each board to show which is which.

1

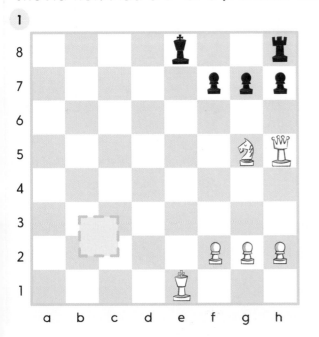

2

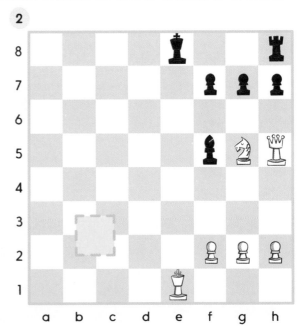

Trapped!

It's possible to trap a castled king behind its own pawns and other pieces. Use a black piece sticker on each board to put White's king in checkmate.

1 Add a black queen.

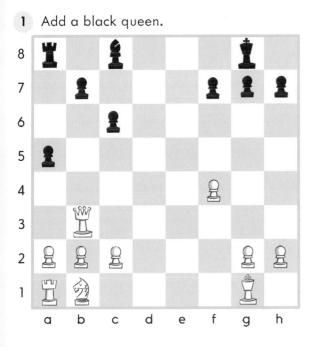

2 Add a black knight.

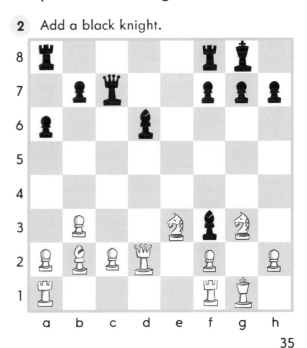

Piece values

Each chess piece is worth a different number of points. The points aren't used for scoring – instead, they tell you which pieces are the most valuable in helping you win the game.

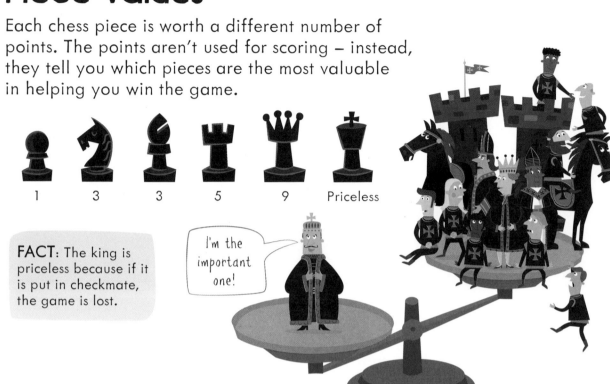

1   3   3   5   9   Priceless

FACT: The king is priceless because if it is put in checkmate, the game is lost.

I'm the important one!

Who has more?

Which player has more points on these boards, Black or White? Write your answers on the dotted lines.

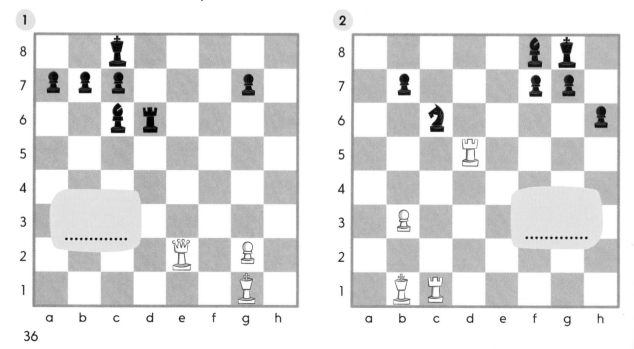

1

2

Balancing act

Add stickers to the right of each = sign to make the sets of pieces equal in value.

 =

 =

3  =

4  =

5 =

6 =

Trading pieces

Sometimes it makes sense to let a piece be captured so you can capture an enemy piece that is worth more points. Put a ✔ sticker by any trades below that would be good for Black, a ✘ sticker by ones that would be bad for Black, and an = sticker by any trades of equal value.

TIP: Pieces can become more or less valuable depending on where they are positioned, and what else is happening in the game.

I thought I was only worth one point...

Ah, but now you're getting a promotion*!

* Read about pawn promotion on page 32.

Chess openings

The first few moves in a game are extremely important. They can have a big influence over who wins and who loses.

You may have the advantage – for now!

Opening tips

- If you're White, you have an advantage: you move first, so you can create threats that Black has to respond to. Try to hold onto this advantage.

- Take control of the central squares on the board.

- Castle early behind a wall of pawns to protect your king.

- Only move two or three pawns on the middle files.

- Try not to move any piece more than once.

- Develop your knights and bishops – this means moving them out so they're ready to attack.

- Don't bring the rooks or the queen out too early.

Opening mistakes

It's possible to win a game of chess in the opening. Draw an arrow on each board to show the move White can make to put Black's king in checkmate.

Who's winning?

The boards below show the end of the opening stage in different games. Which player has developed the pieces better? Write Black or White below each board to show who you think is winning so far.

1

2

TIP: Always remember to play moves that win valuable pieces and avoid playing moves that lose valuable pieces. This gives you the best chance of winning the game.

We're worth more than you!

If only I hadn't been captured...

39

Tactics

Here are some clever tactics that can help you capture pieces.
Look out for your opponent trying to use them too.

Pins

A *pin* is an attack on a piece that is
protecting a more valuable piece.
The protecting piece is pinned
in place – if it moves, the more
valuable piece will be captured.
Draw a circle around each pinned
piece on this board.

Take the bait?

It's Black's turn. Black might be
tempted to make a capture with a
knight – but it's a bad idea. Draw
the move Black shouldn't make
with an arrow, and then draw
another arrow to show White's
next move.

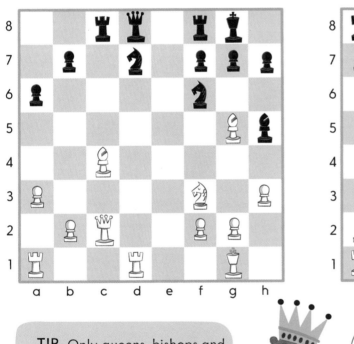

TIP: Only queens, bishops and
rooks can pin enemy pieces.

Hold still...

40

FACT: An *absolute pin* is when a piece is pinned to its king. It is illegal to move that piece because it would put the king in check.

Who's that behind you?

Erm... Nobody...

Pin power

Can you add a white rook sticker to the board below to pin the black queen?

This time, find a way to pin the black queen using a white bishop sticker.

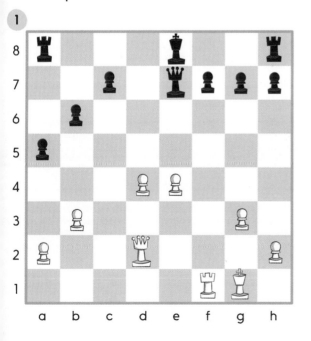

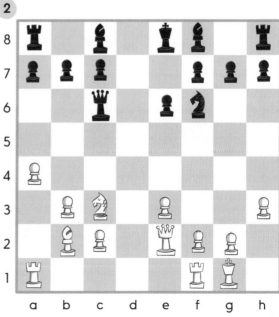

Forks

In each puzzle below, place the piece sticker where it can safely fork (threaten at the same time) two black pieces that aren't pawns.

1 Add a white pawn.

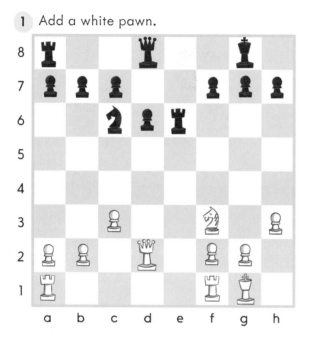

2 Add a white knight.

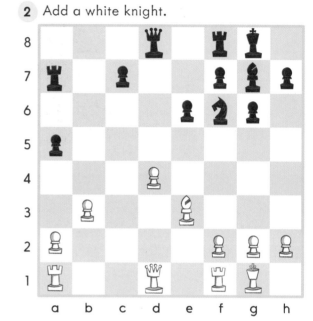

Skewers

A *skewer* is an attack on two pieces at once, in the same direction. The more valuable piece is moved to safety, leaving the less valuable piece for capture. Add a black rook sticker to skewer White's king and rook.

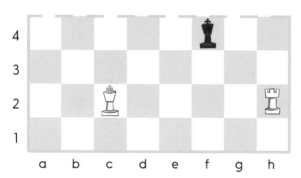

TIP: Even if you get caught by a fork or a skewer, try to look calm and confident. It may make your opponent doubt his or her own plan.

Check!

Do I look worried to you?

Discovered attacks

A *discovered attack* is when a piece moves and uncovers another piece ready to attack. Here's an example:

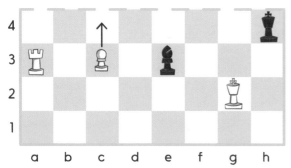

The pawn moves to reveal an attack on the black bishop from the white rook.

The best discovered attacks are when the moved piece also attacks an opponent's piece.

Draw an arrow on the board below to move a White piece into an attacking position, while at the same time creating a discovered attack against another piece.

Surprise!

Discovered check

A *discovered check* is when a piece moves to uncover a check. Draw a safe move White can make below to create a discovered check and threaten another piece at the same time.

HINT: There are two good answers to this puzzle – but one is better than the other...

Thinking ahead

It's useful to keep in mind what your opponent could be planning, and to think about what response you might get to your moves. Thinking ahead will help you thwart your opponent's plans and carry through your own.

> **TIP:** Before you move, ask yourself what move you hope your opponent won't make. Then see if you can place a piece in a position that stops that move from being made.

What happens next?

Draw an arrow on the board below to show Black's move that will make it possible to capture the white bishop in two moves' time.

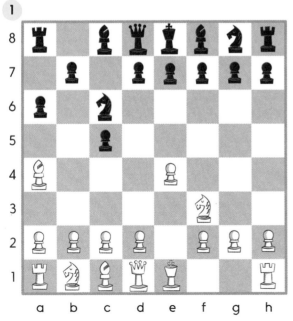

It's White's turn. There is one good move that will lead to an easy victory. Draw it on with an arrow.

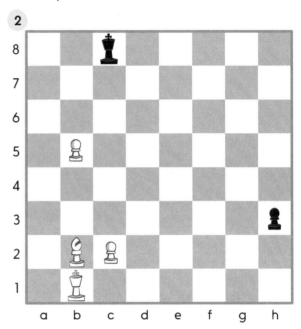

How can White force checkmate in two moves' time? Draw the first move on with an arrow.

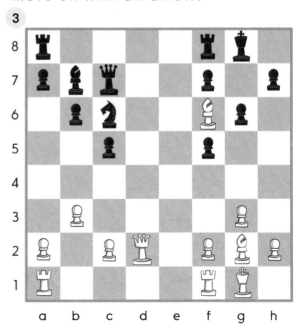

Kings in check

The black king is in check. It has two possible moves. Think about White's response to each, then draw the black king's better move on with an arrow.

TIP: Be flexible. If your opponent makes a move that ruins your plan, you'll need to come up with a new one.

1

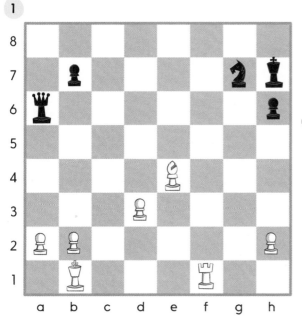

There are only two possible moves Black can make below to get out of check. One move is good, while the other leaves Black vulnerable to checkmate. Draw an arrow on each board to show the good move.

2

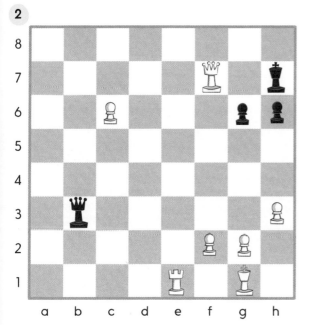

3

Sacrifices

A sacrifice is deliberately letting one of your pieces be captured in order to gain some kind of advantage.

We do appreciate your sacrifice.

I should hope so.

Reasons to make a sacrifice

• It will lead to checkmate.

• It will lead to you capturing pieces of greater value than your sacrifice.

Winning pieces

Here, White is about to make a sacrifice to capture pieces of higher value. Read the descriptions and draw arrows on the board to show the moves. Then, write down the code of the square each piece lands on.

White move 1.
The white queen captures the black bishop. White is deliberately offering the queen as a sacrifice.

Black move 1.
The black king captures the white queen.

White move 2.
The white knight captures a black pawn, forking* the black queen and black king. Black's king is in check.

Black move 2.
The black king **must** move out of check.

White move 3.
The white knight captures the black queen. Both players have now lost their queens, but White is ahead because White also captured a bishop and a pawn.

1 Queen....... King.......   2 Knight....... King....... or ....   3 Knight.......

*You can read about forking on page 24.

Queen sacrifices

On each of these boards White can sacrifice the queen to force checkmate in two moves. Draw arrows to show White's two moves and Black's single move in each case.

I hope there's a good reason for this...

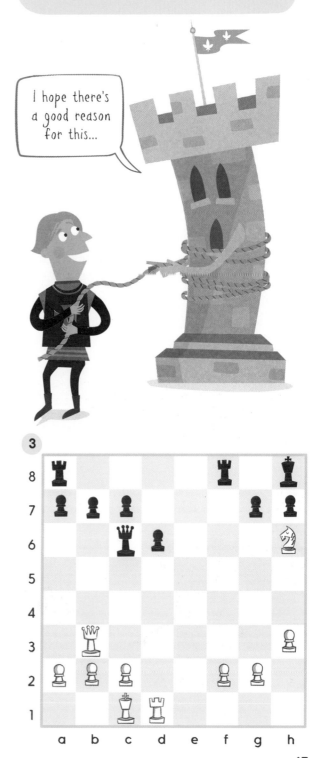

1

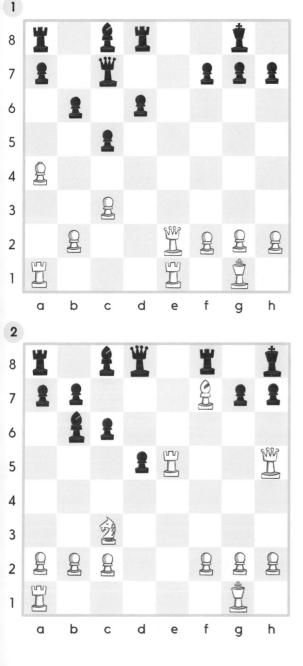

2

3

The endgame

The endgame is the stage of the game where most of the pieces have been captured. Not all games reach this stage.

It's my turn now.

King power

The king can be used as an attacking piece at this stage, as it is safer for it to move around the board. Add a black king sticker to each board below to put the white king in checkmate.

1

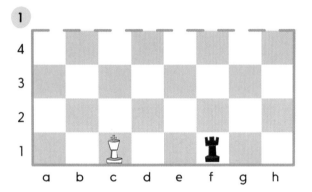

TIP: To make it easier to checkmate your opponent, try to force the king to the edge of the board.

2

3

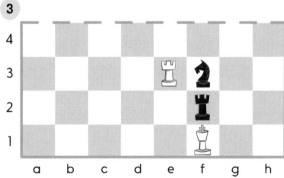

4

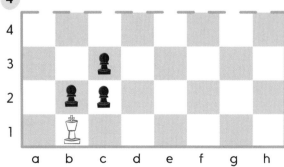

Move!

If I must...

48

Stopping promotion

If your opponent has any pawns left at this stage, you don't want them to be promoted. What single move can White make to stop the black pawn from promoting safely? Draw arrows to show the moves.

1

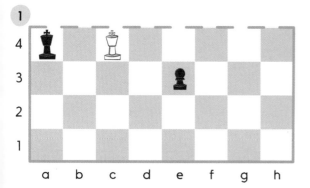

2

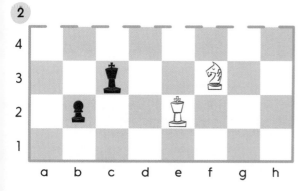

> Don't even think about it...

King in danger

How many ways can the black queen put the white king in checkmate on each of the three boards below? Write the number, then write down the code of each square the queen could move to.

1

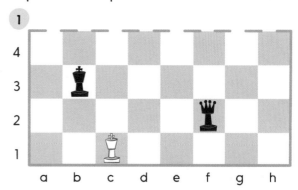

1. ....

2

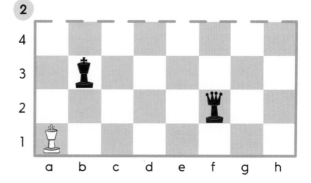

2. ....

3

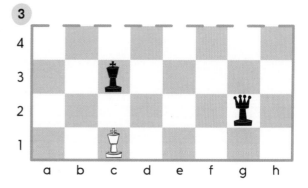

3. ....

It's a draw

A draw usually happens when it looks as if neither side will win, or when it's impossible for either side to win.

We declare a draw!

A draw can happen when...

- it's stalemate – the player whose turn it is has no legal move to make, and is not in check.

- exactly the same position happens three times.

- each player has made 50 moves in a row without a pawn move or a capture.

- neither player has pieces of enough value to checkmate the opponent (see FACT, right).

- both players agree to a draw.

FACT: None of the combinations of pieces below is enough to force checkmate.

A king against:
- a king;
- a king and a bishop;
- a king and one or two knights.

Draw or no draw?

It is better for a player to draw than to lose. It's Black's turn below. Should White agree to a draw? Show your answers with ✓ or ✗ stickers.

1

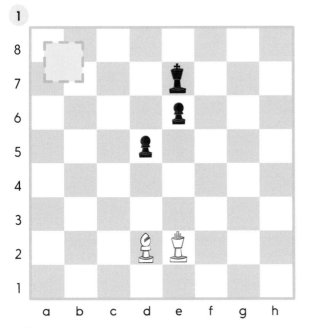

2

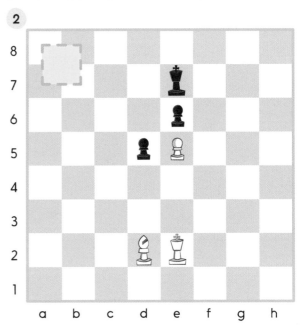

Definite draw?

It's White's turn. Write "Draw" or "Play on" on the boards below to show which set out a definite draw, and which games could continue.

1

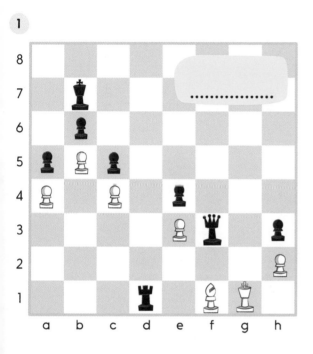

2

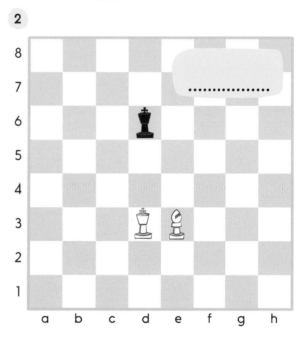

3

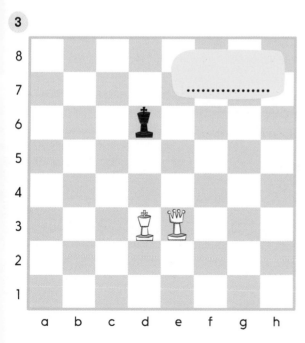

4

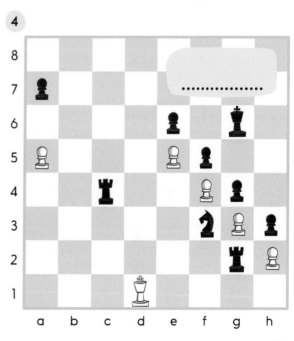

Tricky puzzles

When you've done the rest of the activities in this book, take your chess skills to the next level with these more puzzling challenges.

Pawn puzzles

Use an arrow to show the move that Black should make on each of these boards that will help to promote a pawn safely in a few moves' time.

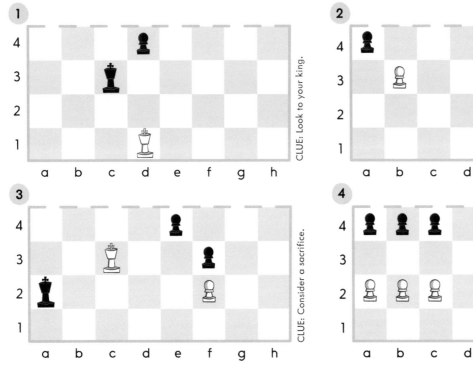

CLUE: Look to your king.

CLUE: Resist temptation.

CLUE: Consider a sacrifice.

CLUE: Move a pawn – but which?

What move should White make to stop Black from promoting the pawn safely? Draw it on with an arrow.

Use an arrow to show the best move for White to make on the board below.

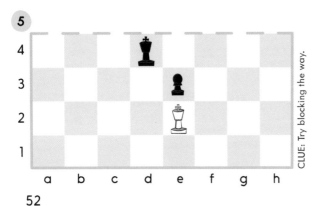

CLUE: Try blocking the way.

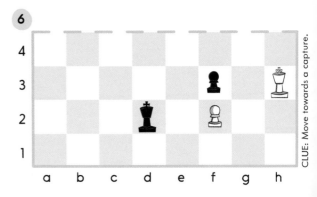

CLUE: Move towards a capture.

Checkmate in two

Checkmate in two is when you make a move and will be able to get checkmate on your next move, no matter what move your opponent makes. Draw White's first move on each board that will give checkmate in two.

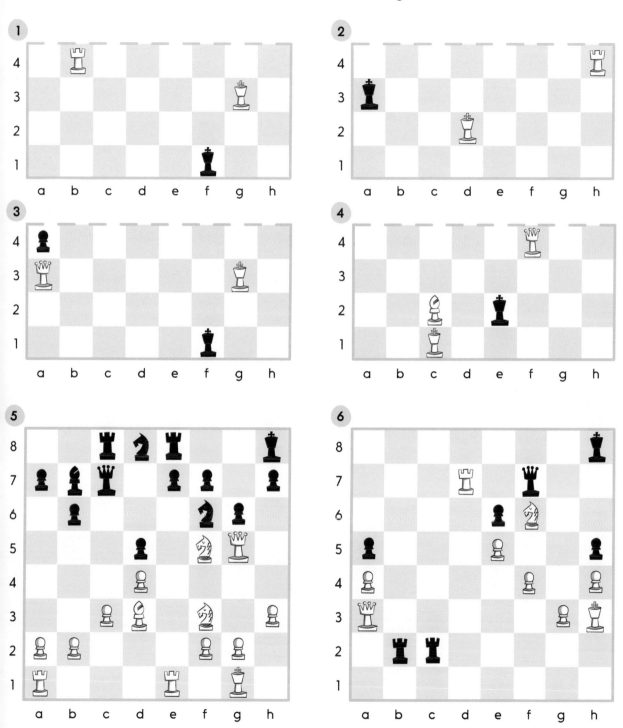

More checkmates in two

Can you spot the move that Black can play on each board to get checkmate in two? Use an arrow to draw the move.

1

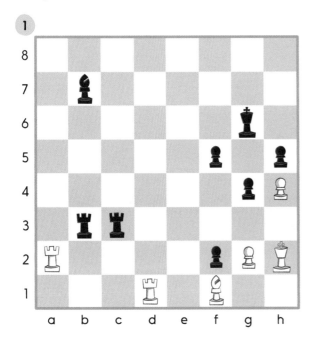

2

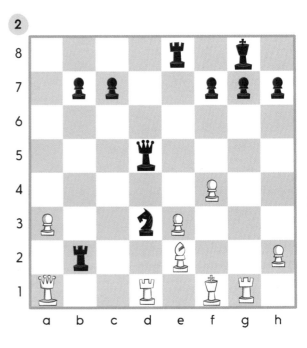

3

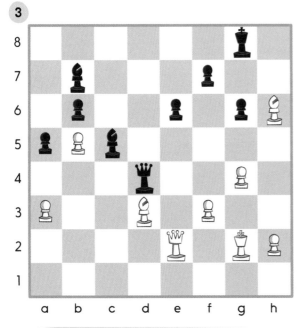

Forced draw

How can Black force a draw here? Show the move with an arrow.

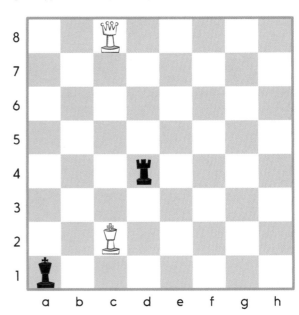

TIP: After Black's move above, there are two moves that White could make next.

White to win

Use an arrow to show White's move that will lead to victory on each board below.

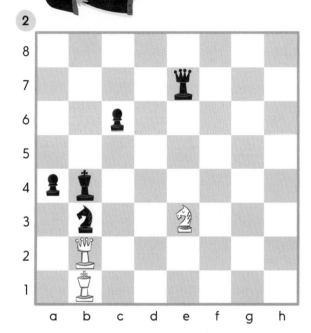
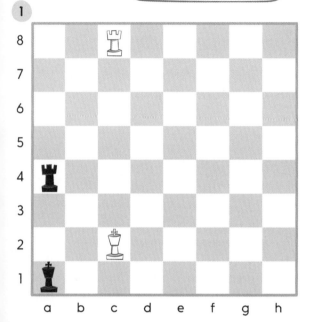
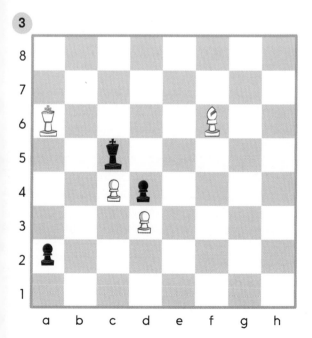
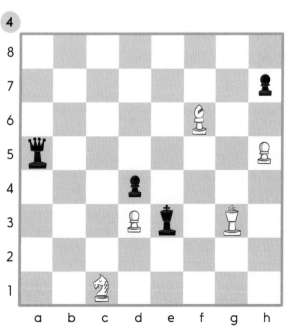

HINT: There is more than one right answer to Piece puzzle and Queen power.

Piece puzzle

Can you place the following white stickers on the board so that none can capture another: two knights, two bishops, two rooks, a queen and a king?

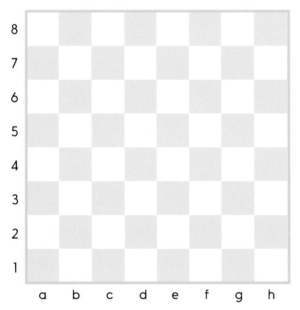

Starting moves

How many opening moves can White choose from? Draw the possible moves on with arrows to help you count them.

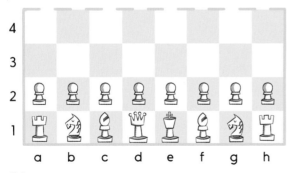

Queen power

Can you place five black queen stickers on this board so that they control every square?

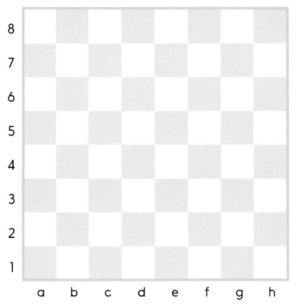

Double attack

What cunning move can White make on the board below to attack two of Black's pieces at once? Draw the move on with arrows.

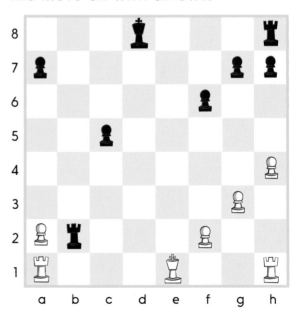

56

Full-house puzzles

How many more of each type of sticker can you place on these boards so that none of the pieces are attacking each other?

HINT: On the answer pages you can find out the maximum number of stickers that will sit on each board – but it's very tricky to fit them all on!

1 white queen

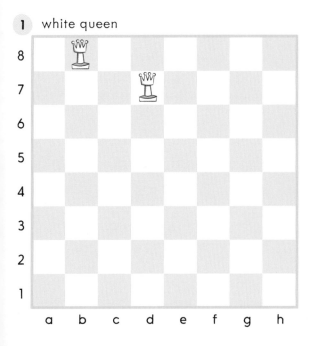

2 black rook

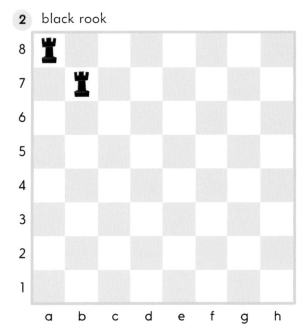

3 white bishop

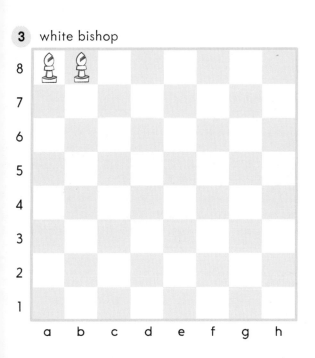

4 black knight

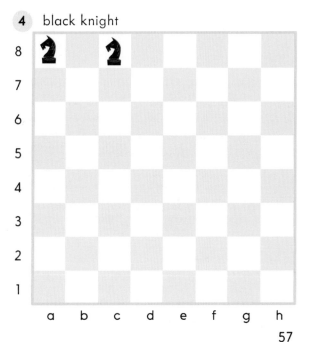

Solutions

4. King moves

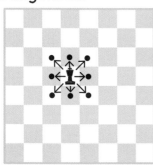

4. Queen moves

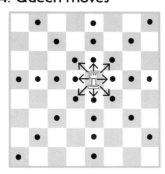

5. Rook moves

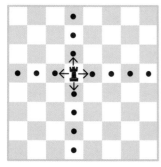

5. Knight moves

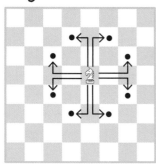

5. Bishop moves

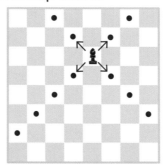

6. Setting up the board

7. Misplaced pieces

7. Areas of the board

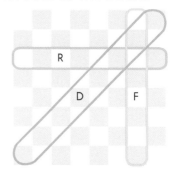

8. Controlling the board

8. Capture!

9. Board codes

	a	b	c	d	e	f	g	h
8	a8	b8	c8	d8	e8	f8	g8	h8
7	a7	b7	c7	d7	e7	f7	g7	h7
6	a6	b6	c6	d6	e6	f6	g6	h6
5	a5	b5	c5	d5	e5	f5	g5	h5
4	a4	b4	c4	d4	e4	f4	g4	h4
3	a3	b3	c3	d3	e3	f3	g3	h3
2	a2	b2	c2	d2	e2	f2	g2	h2
1	a1	b1	c1	d1	e1	f1	g1	h1

9. Pieces in place

Qa5, Bb2, Nc6, Qd4, Ke8, Nf3, Bg7, Rh1

10. Check and checkmate

1. Nd1   2. Qc2   3. Bd2

11. King on the run

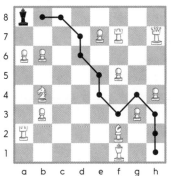

12. Check escape

1. Kf1   2. Be1   3. Knight captures the queen on c1.

13. Checkmate challenges

1. Qh7   2. Re8
3. Bd4   4. Ng7

14. More checkmate challenges

1. Kf3   2. Kd1
3. Kd5   4. Kc1

15. Which is which?

1. Stalemate (White can't legally move.)
2. Checkmate
3. Check (The pawn on g2 can capture the black queen.)
4. Checkmate (The pawn on e2 cannot capture the knight on f3 because it would leave the white king in check from the black queen.)

16. Rook checkmate

1. Rd8   2. Rf8   3. Rg1

17. Rook threats

1. Rb4   2. Rb3

17. Rook attack

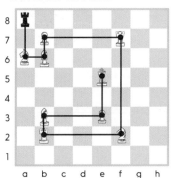

18. Under attack

1. Ba3   2. Qb3
3. Pawn to d5

19. Rook positions

White's rooks are the better positioned because they are on files with no pawns on them. Black's rooks are both trapped behind their own pawns.

19. Teamwork

1. Rf1   2. Ra2 and Rb1

20. Board control

	a	b	c	d	e	f	g	h
8	7	7	7	7	7	7	7	7
7	7	9	9	9	9	9	9	7
6	7	9	11	11	11	11	9	7
5	7	9	11	13	13	11	9	7
4	7	9	11	13	13	11	9	7
3	7	9	11	11	11	11	9	7
2	7	9	9	9	9	9	9	7
1	7	7	7	7	7	7	7	7

20. Piece collecting

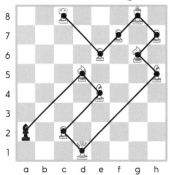

21. Bishop checkmates

1. Bc2 and Bc3
2. Bd3 and Bf2
3. Bg3   4. Bf1

22. Queen in control

	a	b	c	d	e	f	g	h
8	21	21	21	21	21	21	21	21
7	21	23	23	23	23	23	23	21
6	21	23	25	25	25	25	23	21
5	21	23	25	27	27	25	23	21
4	21	23	25	27	27	25	23	21
3	21	23	25	25	25	25	23	21
2	21	23	23	23	23	23	23	21
1	21	21	21	21	21	21	21	21

22. Queen attack

The white queen could capture Rc2, Re7, Ne1, Qh7 and the pawns on b7, c4 and h4.

22. Queen attacked
✗

23. Queen checkmates
1. Qe1   **2.** Qg2   **3.** Qh2
4. Qd3   **5.** Qc2   **6.** Qh1

24. Queen forks
1. Qe6 forks the black rook on b3 and the black king on g4.
2. Qd2 forks the black king on a5 and the black bishop on h2.
3. Qa6 forks the black king on a2 and the black bishop on e6.

25. Runaway queen
Qg1

25. King and queen checkmate
1. Qc2   **2.** Qb3 or Qa1

26. Count the moves

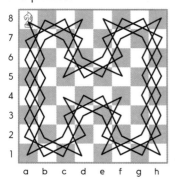

26. Knight tour challenge
This is one way to complete the puzzle:

27. In control

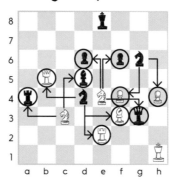

27. Knight journeys
1. 4   **2.** 5

28. Knight captures

28. Sneaky forks
1. Nc6   **2.** Nh6
3. Ne6   **4.** Nd7

29. Checkmates
1. Nf2 and Nh3
2. Nd3 and Ne3

29. Getting to the middle
No ✓

29. Trapped knight
The knight on h8 is trapped.

29. Safe knight
Eight: Rook captures rook on g8, queen captures rook on g8, Kc7, Kc8, Bb6, Be7, Rd5 and Qf6.

30. Pawn protectors
1. Put the white pawn on b3, and the black pawn on d6.
2. Put the white pawn on b2, and the black pawn on b7.

31. Quick pawn quiz
1. c   **2.** b
3. c   **4.** b, b, b

32. Pawn promotion
1. Knight, which checkmates Black. Promoting to a queen, a rook or a bishop would be stalemate.
2. Knight, which forks the black king and queen. Promoting to a queen would draw with best play from Black. Promoting to a rook or a bishop would lose with best play.
3. Rook, which can checkmate Black on its next turn. Promoting to a queen would be stalemate, and promoting to a bishop or a knight would be a draw.

33. Pawn checkmates
1. g3 **2.** c2 **3.** f2 or h2 **4.** d2

33. Think ahead
Kd7, as this will protect the pawn from capture when it moves to e8 to be promoted.

34. Rule breakers?
1. ✗ The king should be on c1 and the rook should be on d1.
2. ✗ The king moved out of check (from the bishop on b4).

35. To castle or not to castle?

1. ✗ The white queen could then capture the black pawn on h7, checkmating Black.
2. ✓ The white queen shouldn't capture the black pawn on h7, because it is protected by the black bishop on f5.

35. Trapped!

1. Qe1   2. Nh3

36. Who has more?

1. Black   2. White

37. Balancing act

1. (Black pawn), black rook, black knight, black pawn.
2. White king.
3. (Black rook), black rook, black bishop.
4. White pawn, white knight.
5. (Black king), black knight.
6. White bishop, white rook, white pawn.

37. Trading pieces

1. ✓ A rook is worth more than a bishop.
2. ✗ A knight is worth less than a rook.
3. ═ A bishop is worth the same as a knight.

38. Opening mistakes

1. Qh5   2. Qf7

39. Who's winning?

1. White: White's pieces are controlling the central squares and the king is safely castled. Black has moved the king into danger, moved side pawns and developed the rooks too soon.
2. Black: Black's pieces are well developed and the king is safely castled. White has moved side pawns and developed the rooks too soon.

40. Pins

Bc4, Nf3, Nf6, pawn on f7 and Nd7

40. Take the bait?

Black shouldn't capture the white knight on d5 with the black knight on f6, because then the white bishop on g5 can capture the black queen on d8.

41. Pin power

1. Re5   2. Bb5

42. Forks

1. A white pawn on d5 forks Nc6 and Re6.
2. A white knight on c6 forks Ra7 and Qd8.

42. Skewers

Ra2

43. Discovered attacks

Bb5 uncovers an attack by the white queen on the black queen, while at the same time putting the black king in check.

43. Discovered check

Nc6 or Ng6. Nc6 is the better move because it will lead to the white knight capturing the black queen, whereas Ng6 would lead to it capturing the black rook.

44. What happens next?

1. Black moves a pawn to b5, threatening the white bishop on a4. The bishop then moves to b3 to escape. Black then moves another pawn to c4, and now the bishop can't escape capture.
2. White moves a bishop to e5 to stop the black pawn from advancing towards promotion.
3. White moves the queen to h6. Black can't stop the queen from moving to g7 on the next move, which is checkmate.

45. Kings in check

1. Kg8 is better than Kh8. (After Kh8, White could checkmate Black with Rf8.)
2. Qf7 (capturing the white queen) is better than Kh8. (After Kh8, White could checkmate Black with Re8.)
3. Pawn to d5 is better than Kf8. (After Kf8, White could checkmate Black with Bh6.)

46. Winning pieces

1. Queen h8, King h8
2. Knight f7, King g7 or g8
3. Knight d8

47. Queen sacrifices

1. The white queen moves to e8, putting the black king in check. The black rook on d8 captures the white queen. The white rook on e1 then captures the black rook on e8, checkmating Black.

2. The white queen captures the black pawn on h7, putting the black king in check. The black king captures the white queen. The white rook on e5 then moves to h5, checkmating Black.

3. The white queen moves to g8, putting the black king in check. The black rook on f8 captures the white queen. The white knight moves to f7, checkmating Black.

48. King power

1. Kc3   **2.** Kc4
3. Kg3   **4.** Kb3

49. Stopping promotion

1. Kd3
2. Nd2

49. King in danger

1. 2 ways: e1 or c2
2. 5 ways: e1, f1, g1, b2 and a2
3. 4 ways: c2, f1, g1 and h1

50. Draw or no draw?

1. ✔ Even with best play, White can only draw against Black.
2. ✗ With best play, White can eventually capture the black pawns, then promote its own pawn and force checkmate.

51. Definite draw?

1. Draw (It is stalemate, because White can't move.)
2. Draw (Neither player has enough pieces for checkmate.)
3. Play on (White could checkmate Black.)
4. Play on (White must move the pawn from a5 to a6. Then, Black can checkmate White by moving the rook to d2.)

52. Pawn puzzles

1. Kd3 (The white king must move to c1 or e1. The black king then moves to c2 or e2, where it can protect the promoting square.)   **2.** Pawn to a3   **3.** Pawn to e3
4. Pawn to b3 (White is likely to capture this pawn with one of its own. Black doesn't capture but instead moves the pawn whose file is blocked. White's next move will clear a path to promotion for one of the pawns.)   **5.** Ke1   **6.** Kg4

53. Checkmate in two

1. The white rook moves to e4. The black king must move to g1. The white rook then moves to e1, checkmating Black.
2. The white king moves to c2. The black king must then move to a2. The white rook then moves to a4, checkmating Black.
3. The white queen moves to e3. The black pawn moves towards promotion on a3. The white queen then moves to f2, checkmating Black.

4. The white queen moves to g3. Black's king must move to f1. The white bishop then moves to d3, checkmating Black.
5. The white queen captures the black knight on f6, putting the black king in check. *Then, either:* the black pawn on e7 captures the white queen, and the white rook captures the black rook on e8, checkmating Black. *Or:* the black king moves to g8 and the white queen moves to g7, checkmating Black.
6. The white queen moves to f8, putting the black king in check. *Then, either:* the black queen captures the white queen, and the white rook moves to h7, checkmating Black. *Or:* the black queen moves to g8, then the white queen captures the black queen, putting Black in checkmate.

54. More checkmates in two

1. The black rook on c3 moves to h3, putting the white king in check. The white pawn on g2 captures the black rook. The black pawn on g4 then moves to g3, working with the black bishop on b7, checkmating White.
2. The black queen moves to f3, putting the white king in check. The white bishop must then capture the black queen. The black rook moves to f2, checkmating White.
3. The black queen captures the white pawn on g4, putting the white king in check. The white king must then move to f1 or h1. The black queen then moves to g1, checkmating White.

54. Forced draw

The black rook moves to c4, forking the white king and white queen. The white queen then captures the black rook. This is then stalemate, because Black has no legal moves.

55. White to win

1. The white king moves to b3. If the black rook then moves to safety, the white rook can move to c1 and checkmate Black.

2. The white queen moves to a3, skewering the black king and queen. If the black king then captures the white queen, the white knight will move to c2 and checkmate Black.

3. The white king moves to b7. If the black pawn moves to a1 to promote, the white bishop can move to e7, checkmating Black.

4. The white bishop captures the black pawn on d4, putting Black in check. The black king then captures the white bishop or moves to d2. The white knight can then move to b3, forking Black's king and queen. Once Black's queen is captured, the white knight can capture Black's pawn on h7, enabling White's pawns to promote.

56. Piece puzzle

This is one solution to the puzzle:

56. Queen power

This is one way of answering the puzzle:

56. Starting moves

20. The white pawns can all move one square or two (16 moves in total), and the two white knights each have two possible moves.

56. Double attack

The white king and white rook on a1 castle. This threatens the black rook on b2 and the black king.

57. Full-house puzzles

1. (white queens) 8 is the maximum number of queens that will fit. This is one way to arrange them:

2. (black rooks) 8 is the maximum number of rooks that will fit. This is one way to arrange them:

3. (white bishops) 14 is the maximum number of bishops that will fit. This is one way to arrange them:

4. (black knights) 32 is the maximum number of knights that will fit. This is how to arrange them:

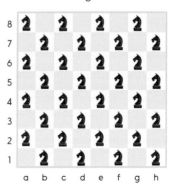

Index

Acknowledgements

Additional design by Joanne Kirkby and Karen Tomlins

Stickers

6. Setting up the board

10. Check and checkmate

13. Checkmate challenges

14. More checkmate challenges

16. Rook checkmate

19. Teamwork

21. Bishop checkmates

22. Queen attacked

✓ ✗

23. Queen checkmates

24. Queen forks

28. Sneaky forks

29. Checkmates

30. Pawn protectors

33. Pawn checkmates

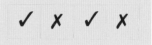

34. Rule breakers?

✓ ✗ ✓ ✗

35. To castle or not to castle?

✓ ✗

35. Trapped!

37. Balancing act

1

2

3

37. Balancing act

4			
5			
6			

37. Trading pieces

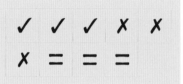

41. Pin power

42. Forks

42. Skewers

48. King power

50. Draw or no draw?

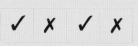

56. Piece puzzle

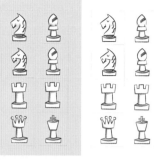

56. Queen power

57. Queen puzzle

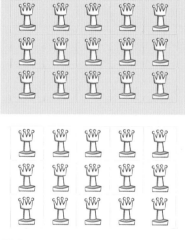

57. Rook puzzle

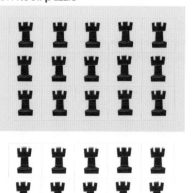

57. Bishop puzzle

57. Knight puzzle